THE SECRET LIFE OF SPIES

WIDE EYED EDITIONS

Espionage is one of the oldest human activities ever to have existed. Spies from across the globe have shaped and changed the world, often in surprising ways. Although they try to keep their work hidden from everyday view, they have left their impact scattered throughout history. This gives us a chance to look inside the mysterious world of spies and uncover some of the incredible techniques they use in their inscrutable work.

We know that spies have been at work since ancient times, thanks to their appearance in age-old stories. Accounts of their adventures made thrilling tales, while historians pored over the details to uncover the invaluable role played by these individuals in conflicts. Over time, spies developed a reputation for cunning and secrecy. Soon, espionage became one of the most important tools used by military leaders. Spies also acted as explorers, applying their skills in secrecy and observation to discover whatever they could about new territories and rival civilizations. As their roles became more complex, spies started to work as part of powerful and hidden organizations that could make or break a leader. Today, espionage organizations work in international networks, while doing their best to keep what they do firmly hidden in the shadows.

Spanning history and traveling across borders, this book will reveal a kaleidoscope of agents who dedicated their lives to the world of espionage. We will embark on a journey through the incredible history of spies, from the earliest accounts of espionage in ancient China right up to our modern globalized society, to discover how spies work in today's fast-paced and ever-changing world. On the way, we will meet some of the real men and women who operated in the shadows to gather intelligence, disrupt their enemies, and steal secrets.

This is the secret life of spies.

There are many different kinds of spy and several types of espionage. However, the one thing they all have in common is the control of intelligence. For spies, the word "intelligence" does not simply mean "cleverness." It is a specific term that refers to knowledge about a situation. The commander of an army will want to know how many soldiers are fighting for the enemy and where they are located. A business leader will be more successful if she knows what her competitors are planning. All of this useful information is known as intelligence, and it is the job of the spy to discover it.

Of course, not all spies steal secrets. Some spies work to prevent enemies from spying on them. They spend their time gathering information on enemy spies so that they can hunt them down and stop them. Sometimes they give them false information to confuse and thwart their plans. This is called "counterintelligence" and is some of the most difficult work for any spy to do. This is because counterintelligence pits spy against spy, with each side doing its very best to defeat the other.

The world of spies is often thought to be incredibly fascinating and dramatic—in fiction, spies are often presented as mysterious and deadly, with action-packed adventures around every corner. However, the real life of a spy can be very different. Good spies blend in with their surroundings and do their best to look just like everybody else. The less attention they draw to themselves, the better!

The ideal spy will be the last person you would expect to be involved in the world of espionage. For this reason, some of the best spies have been, and still are, women. This is because, traditionally, women were not expected to be involved in military matters. Of course, this is ridiculous, and women make just as good members of the military as men. But in this instance, this prejudice toward women could be used to a spy's advantage. In the past, few people expected a woman to be a spy, which meant they could carry out their work unnoticed and without any suspicion from their enemies.

Espionage can be dangerous work, especially in times of war. Good intelligence is extremely valuable, which means that spies are highly respected by their own side. However, it also means that they are utterly hated by their opponents. Their work often takes them into enemy territory and being captured is a constant threat. Some of the spies in this book were caught, imprisoned, and even killed for their actions. Many of them faced their punishment with great bravery, remaining committed to their mission to the very end.

The spies at greatest risk are those who betray their own side by passing intelligence to their country's rivals or competitors. These spies, called double agents, often operate undetected for years but, if caught, are labeled as traitors.

Fictional spies, like James Bond, are often shown using super-high-tech gadgets to help them in their missions, and although this make-believe equipment is often pretty far-fetched, real spies do in fact make use of the latest technology to help them with their work! Spies have used secret codes, hidden compartments in everyday objects such as pens and umbrellas, and tiny cameras to capture images. In today's world, telecommunications are a key tool of espionage and spies listen in to phone conversations, monitor internet use, and even use orbiting satellites to gather intelligence. This means that modern espionage costs a lot of money, and governments devote a lot of time and energy to ensuring that their spies have the resources needed to do their jobs effectively.

However, even the most technologically-equipped spies of the 21st century have the same core mission as their counterparts from ancient times. **They gather, divert and conceal information, steal secrets, and always try to stay one step ahead of their enemies.**

This is their story.

Aphra Behn

1640–1689 born: England

I'm one of the most famous playwrights in the country. I'm a supporter of the monarchy and I know the king, Charles II, personally.

He's the most powerful man in the land, and yet he's probably one of the most scared—he has enemies everywhere. His father, the old king, was murdered by "Parliamentarians," who thought the monarchy was bad for the country. They believe that Parliament, not the king, should have power. They are very serious about it too. They executed the old king in 1649 when Charles was still a teenager. Charles escaped to France until he was able to return to England to take up the crown that was rightfully his. However, he has never felt truly safe and worries that the Parliamentarians will bring him down like they did his father.

The king also has enemies abroad, and our country has been at war with the Dutch several times. The difficulty in dealing with enemies in your own country is that there is nothing to distinguish them from your friends. However, it also creates an opportunity. If Englishmen who have been conspiring against Charles II can instead be made to support him in secret, they could be very useful. It was for this reason that in August 1666 I was sent to Antwerp on a mission to find out as much as I could about Englishmen plotting against the king. I knew that some of them were working with other traitors and even providing help to the king's Dutch enemies. I was given code names "Astrea" and "Agent 160," and had £50 (nearly $13,000 in today's money) to spend on my mission.

I sent reports of my progress to my handler in England, Thomas Killigrew. We were both worried that our enemies would intercept the messages, so used a special cipher to disguise them. While in Holland, I met William Scott, whose father had been one of the men responsible for executing the old king. He was serving in a regiment of English traitors on the Dutch side. I found out that he needed money and wanted an official pardon for opposing the king. This was a perfect opportunity to turn him into a double agent.

Creating a double agent is a delicate matter. The king would need to be able to trust that the agent had been truly "turned" and that they were not simply pretending to help him while continuing to pass information to his enemies. Secrecy was essential. We were both in danger if we got caught, so I asked him to take a long journey with me so that we could speak without fear of being overheard. We traveled for an entire day, and although he was shy at first, I was able to convince him.

I asked my handler, Killigrew, to obtain a royal pardon for Scott. And to show good faith on his part, Scott passed information to us about a group plotting against the king. However, Scott's pardon still hadn't come through and the money that I had been given to carry out my mission was nearly all gone. Scott, too, was short of money, and eventually he was put in prison for not paying his debts. Without him, I had no source of useful intelligence, and I had to abandon my mission. I was glad to get back to England, but disappointed that the king didn't pay me for my work. I turned things around though and began to make a living as a writer. It is as an author that I am best known, but I'll never forget my short career as a spy.

Code names

• Code names are secret labels that spies use when communicating with their handlers. They are used to prevent too many people from finding out the spy's real name and identity. Some code names resemble ordinary names, while others are straightforward codes and might be part of a pattern. Aphra Behn had one of each type: "Astrea" and "Agent 160." The most famous spy code name is that of James Bond, who is code-named 007. In James Bond's fictional world, the 00 classification (pronounced "double O") means that the officer is licensed to kill.

Sun Tzu

545–470 BCE born: China

I am a Chinese military commander and the author of one of the most important works about achieving military success, *The Art of War*.
This manual provides guidance on how to win battles. It is not about how to fight—combat is unpredictable and comes at a high cost. I believe it is better to win by avoiding actual battles and simply outsmarting your opponents instead. *"All warfare is based on deception."*

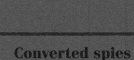

Deception requires intelligence. Imagine you are a military commander and you intend to deceive your enemy. Unless you already have intelligence on them, you cannot even begin to do this. You need to be able to transmit false information and create diversions. If you are weak, convince the enemy you are strong. If your forces are in disorder, make it look as though you are disciplined. The point is always to be better informed than your enemies.

Local spies
These are ordinary people from the enemy's own land or district, from whom you obtain information. You can do this by getting them to tell you information (by force if necessary) or by simply observing them.

Inside spies
Staff and soldiers from the enemy's own side, who give you information while continuing to work for the enemy. These agents can be very effective, especially if they have access to secret information through their work.

Converted spies
This is when an enemy's own spies are recruited to work for your side while pretending to remain loyal to the enemy, becoming "double agents." They are similar to inside agents and can provide secret information from the opposing side. Since the enemy expects them to spy on you, you can give them false information to deceive their handlers.

The Art of War *and spycraft*

•   Although *The Art of War* is attributed to Sun Tzu, some scholars are not convinced that he actually wrote it. However, regardless of who the author is, it continues to be regarded as an important and influential piece of work.

•   *The Art of War* aims to avoid combat and for this reason has been taken as advice for any competitive situation. Business leaders, politicians, and sports coaches have described it as a useful source of advice in their fields.

•   The book was written at a particular time in history and at a specific location. However, its analysis is written in a general way that makes it easy to apply in different situations, especially for spies. Every spy that you meet in this book fits into one or more of Sun Tzu's categories. Can you figure out which one applies to each person?

Whether you are gathering intelligence or creating deceptions, you need spies. *The Art of War* describes five types of spy, and although the book is around 2,500 years old, every single one of these types is still used by intelligence agencies today. You cannot afford to ignore any one of them. Remember, you are not only spying on and seeking to deceive your enemy, your enemy is spying on and seeking to deceive you. It is difficult to know who to trust in the world of spies. I call the use of all five types of spy the "Golden Skein," though modern spies call it "multi-source intelligence."

Doomed spies

These are agents from your side who you employ to deliberately create false information or act in a way designed to confuse your enemies and prevent them from spying on you accurately. If they are discovered, they will be killed, so they are called "doomed" or "dead" spies.

Living spies

These are your own spies who you send to observe the enemy and bring back intelligence to help you. They may travel to your enemy's territory without being seen or they may travel under a false identity.

孫子兵法

Mary Bowser

c. 1846-unkown born: USA

Bowser is my married name. I was born Mary Jane Richards and have used several different names in my life; Mary Garvin, Richmonia Richards, Richmonia St. Pierre. Names come and go—it's all part of my disguise. As a girl, I was the property of John Van Lew and his wife, Eliza. African Americans like me were kept as slaves by white owners and forced to work without pay. It was usually a lifelong situation and many slaves were born into it. However, in 1865, it was made illegal nationwide by the Thirteenth Amendment to the Constitution, and I'm proud to say that I helped to end this horrific practice.

Van Lew's daughter, Elizabeth, took control of her family's business after her father died. Elizabeth hated slavery and was an "abolitionist" (someone who campaigned to make slavery illegal). She released me from slavery and ensured I got an education. But it was difficult even with my newfound freedom. In the 1860s, the country went to war with itself. The Confederacy, made up of pro-slavery states, chose to leave the United States rather than give up slavery. The war was between them and the Union—states from the north that had already abolished slavery and wanted all states to do the same. Elizabeth and I were in favor of the Union, but we lived in Virginia, a Confederate state.

Elizabeth knew Varina Davis, the wife of Jefferson Davis, who was the president of the Confederate States. Varina needed someone to clean and tidy her house. I took the job, and as I carried out my duties, I had access to all sorts of documents, maps, and letters and heard many of Davis's plans. As a black woman, I was almost entirely invisible to them. They believed I had no education and didn't bother covering up any documents. None of them ever imagined that I could even read. How wrong they were.

Elizabeth ran a network of spies called the Richmond Underground. As a wealthy white woman, she had access to many of the leading figures on the Confederate side, and her spies stole secrets and sent them to Union generals to help them win the war. She asked me to join the spy ring, which I agreed to immediately. One of our main challenges was keeping our messages secret. We used ciphers to disguise our writing and devised ingenious ways of hiding notes. To pass information, I sewed messages into the hems of dresses and gave them to another spy. To signal that the message was ready, I hung a red shirt on the clothesline outside.

With so much intelligence finding its way to the Union, Davis grew suspicious. The house was put on high alert and everyone—including me—became a suspect. I had to get out, but it wasn't as easy as walking out of the door. As soon as I left, Davis would know that I was the spy and send people after me. I had to sneak out. I took my chance, hid on the back of a wagon, and found my way to safety. In the end, the Union won the war and slavery was outlawed. It is remembered as a military conflict, but I would say that my hidden role was a big part of securing victory. I'm glad to have been able to do so much.

Drops

- The exchange of information between two spies is called a "drop." These fall into two types: a "live drop" is when the contacts meet in person to exchange information; a "dead drop" is when the contacts don't meet in person and take an alternative method to exchange their information.

- In some cases, the deposit of the materials is followed by a signal from one spy to another, informing them to come and collect them. In other cases, a spy often leaves material at a given location and their contact periodically visits the same location to see if any material is there.

- Mary and Elizabeth used a form of dead drop when they passed messages sewn into dresses, with a red shirt acting as the signal.

- There are risks with using a dead drop. A third party may interfere with the materials in the time between them being dropped and being picked up. This could be an innocent person simply removing them, or it could be an enemy who chooses to deliberately interfere with them.

- For this reason, many dead drops are disguised as ordinary items, such as rocks. Remember, all good spies will take care to use encryption wherever possible.

Sir Francis Walsingham

c. 1532–1590   born: England

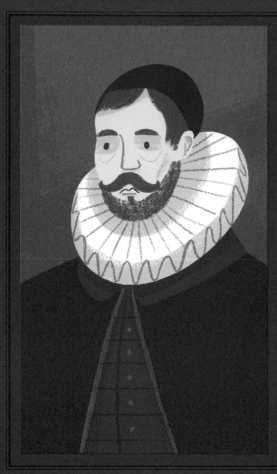

I know every plot, every scheme, and every plan that is going on in the kingdom. It is my job to know these things and—even more importantly—to control them.

I am Sir Francis Walsingham, spymaster to Queen Elizabeth I of England. Be under no illusion, I am one of the most powerful people in the country. Officially, I am Her Majesty's foreign secretary, responsible for managing her relations with the rulers of other countries. However, my work is somewhat more important than that and rather more secret. In truth, I have two responsibilities: to protect the queen and to preserve the Protestant faith.

My two priorities are linked. Her Majesty is a Protestant, the defender of the faith in England, while her enemies are mostly Catholic. There are people at home and abroad who would like nothing more than to remove Queen Elizabeth from the throne and replace her with a Catholic monarch. Luckily for Her Majesty, I am a *very* effective spymaster. My approach is always to assume danger. It is a fatal error to underestimate one's enemies, and I never make that mistake.

I have agents called "intelligencers" all over Europe. Some of them I directly employ, others are in the service of rival powers, but all of them have a secret loyalty to me. They supply me with information about what is going on in foreign courts. I rely on two types of information, which future spymasters will describe as human intelligence and signals intelligence. For me, it simply means using informers to tell me secrets and intercepting letters so that I can read them. I never rely on just one source and I'm careful to compare information from different agents.

Intelligence gathering disciplines

• Modern spies use several "intelligence gathering disciplines," which are based on the type of source they use. Many of these disciplines have been used since ancient times, but these days are given six-letter names ending in "INT" for "intelligence."

• The two most commonly used are human intelligence (HUMINT) and signals intelligence (SIGINT). HUMINT is material gathered from a person—captured soldiers or agents on the ground for example. SIGINT is gathered from intercepted communications and uses old techniques (such as intercepting letters) and modern methods, including tapping phone lines and tracking a target's internet activity.

The greatest of the queen's enemies is her cousin Mary, Queen of Scots, who believes she is entitled to the throne of England. Knowing that Mary and her French husband, Philip, were likely to be planning something, I intercepted letters between them. It is important to gather intelligence without it being noticed. My employee Arthur Gregory has a talent for breaking and repairing letter seals, so—thanks to him—I could read the letters and send them to their destination without anyone suspecting a thing. Some of the letters were encrypted or written in code, but my cryptographer Thomas Phelippes can decipher any code.

I arranged for Mary to be imprisoned in the custody of a friend who operated under my strict instructions. These included blocking every method for Mary to send secret letters. Every method . . . except one. Some of Mary's letters were smuggled out in a beer keg, which she believed to be totally secret. Little did she know I had complete control of this. Her conspirator, Anthony Babington, wrote to Mary about a scheme to assassinate the queen and I intercepted Mary's reply. This was written in cipher, but Phelippes cracked it in less than a day. Mary had given her approval for Babington to launch his plot against Elizabeth. I gave Elizabeth a copy and urged her to act against her Catholic rival. The queen was hesitant, but I applied pressure. She is perhaps not as ruthless as I am, but that is what she employs me for. She owes me her life.

Andrew Parker

1962– born: UK

My name is Andrew Parker and I've made a career as an intelligence officer. I have been director general of Britain's Security Service, better known as MI5, since 2013.

It gives me great pride to lead a professional organization that is committed to the security of the nation. Unlike many people involved in espionage, I don't use a false identity or disguise. In fact, my appointment as director general is publicly acknowledged by the government. But this wasn't always the case—for a very long time the very existence of MI5 and the name of its director general was a matter of secrecy. These days things are very different, and my name and photograph even appear on the agency's website!

At MI5, our main responsibilities are to combat terrorism and to prevent hostile countries and organizations from spying in the UK. MI5 is over a hundred years old and has focused on eliminating threats to the country throughout its existence—threats that have changed over time. In the two world wars, the chief threat was Germany and MI5 officers worked tirelessly to track down German agents. However, for most of the organization's lifetime, its principal concern was the Soviet Union. Although we were never officially at war with the Soviets, a deep mistrust existed between our countries and we spent our time seeking out Soviet agents. But this all came to an end when the Soviet Union collapsed in the 1990s. Since then, our main role has been in the fight against terrorism.

Like all espionage organizations, we use a range of different sources and methods to help us. We try to avoid revealing too much about our techniques so that our targets cannot benefit from the knowledge. We also have to adapt to stay ahead and respond to the challenges of a changing world. One thing that stays the same is that we use "covert human intelligence sources," or in other words, agents. These are not employees of MI5, but are usually people with a connection to an organization we have an interest in and who can supply us with secret information.

Spies in other fields

- The methods and techniques of espionage are used in many fields. Businesses sometimes engage in "industrial espionage," where they spy on competitors to steal their ideas. Some companies even ask their staff to take jobs at a rival firm so that they can retrieve information, while others have been known to break into rival businesses to steal information directly.

- There are spies in the world of sports, too. Teams and clubs have been known to send staff to observe their rivals secretly so that they can understand their sporting tactics and gather intelligence on the condition of the players. In 2019, English soccer club Leeds United was caught sending a spy to observe their rivals Derby County. After they were exposed, Leeds admitted that they had spied on every club in their league, which was against the rules.

Some of our surveillance work uses technology to allow us to listen in on phone calls and track internet activity. We even gather communications data in bulk, which means that it includes data from thousands of people, many of whom have nothing to do with our investigations. However, bulk data allows us to look for patterns of activity that help us to identify our targets. This isn't always a popular method, and people criticize us for it. But my staff always take care to use the right amount of surveillance and to respect the right to privacy wherever possible. Any intrusive surveillance has to be approved by a cabinet minister. This can be a challenge, as it adds delays and our work is often fast moving.

It is a fine balance, and our work goes beyond what would be permitted for the average person. My staff is allowed to break certain laws if it means they can make a real breakthrough in an investigation. We try to avoid this wherever we can, but for me the security of the country is paramount.

Bertrandon de la Broquière

c. 1400–1459 born: France

I'm the "Premier Écuyer Tranchant," which is French for "First Squire" to Duke Philip the Good, the ruler of the Duchy of Burgundy.

My life in Philip's service has been successful, and I'm glad to have had the opportunity to work for him. My long relationship with Philip means that I have earned his trust, and it was for this reason that he sent me out on a secret mission.

People from Christian territories like mine have been fighting with people in Muslim territories for hundreds of years. Our wars are as much the result of political disagreements as anything else. A series of Muslim rulers took control of Anatolia (later known as Turkey) and began to build a powerful realm called the Ottoman Empire. The growing power of this empire made many rulers (including Philip) uneasy, and they wanted to find out as quickly as they could how they could take it down. Discovering this was my secret mission.

Legends

•   Spies who work in enemy or foreign territory sometimes make up a cover story that explains what they are doing there in the event that the spy is captured—this is called a "legend." Bertrandon told people that he was a simple pilgrim while he was secretly carrying out espionage work. Some spies adopt entirely false identities as part of their legend and effectively live their lives undercover. Their agencies provide them with fake documents and even stage family photographs to make an effective legend.

I set out disguised as a pilgrim (someone who visits a holy place for religious reasons). I traveled some of the way with other pilgrims, which helped with my deception, and it was also much safer to travel with companions. Our route took us by boat from Europe to the Middle East. We pressed on into the Sinai Desert, but I fell ill and changed my route instead to Beirut and Damascus. I was secretly making observations of the defenses available in each town. I kept a special eye out for weak spots and places that would be particularly vulnerable to attack.

I set out to return to Burgundy, passing through the heartlands of the Ottoman Empire. This, I was told, would be impossible for a Christian. My journey would be filled with potential enemies. I was wary, but I disguised myself in the local costume and employed a man named Mohammed to act as my guide. He helped me navigate through the customs and traditions of the region. We passed through many towns ruined by warfare, including some that had been home to Christians before the Ottomans took over. It was a reminder that my mission was critical.

Later, I met a man named Benedict Folco, who had been sent by the Duke of Milan to meet the Sultan of the Ottoman Empire. With Benedict, I would be able to enter the royal palace. I had the chance to observe the Sultan, speak to his staff, and gather the information about his defenses. Carefully and very secretly, I made notes of how many soldiers the Sultan had, the types of weapon they used, and looked for any weak spots. I noticed, with great horror, that the Sultan had enough power to invade Europe if he wanted. I didn't know if this was his plan, but I concentrated my work on how to defend against him if he did. It would be for Philip to decide what to do with my intelligence.

Hedy Lamarr

1914–2000 born: Austria

I'm not a spy. Far from it. I'm a famous actress, which is the last thing any spy wants to be.

But despite my success in the movies I'd prefer to be remembered for my talents as an inventor. And it is because of these talents that I entered into the world of espionage. I've always had a knack for solving technical problems. My ex-husband Friedrich was an arms dealer, and I used to listen in on his business conversations. He'd talk about the machines and special equipment that were used to make weapons. Friedrich supported the Nazis, but I intended to use my skills to support the Allied side in the war. I suppose, when you think about it, I was a spy, listening in to his conversations and using the intelligence to thwart him.

I found his weapons talk fascinating. The technical problems that need to be solved when looking at them in detail amazed me. I found the radio signals that ships and aircraft use particularly interesting. Torpedoes were controlled by these signals, so they could be aimed with precision. However, radio signals are very easy to jam. It doesn't matter how sophisticated your torpedo is; if the enemy can jam the signal, then it will be impossible to control.

However, to me, the problem seemed very easy to solve. All it would require was making radio signals undetectable or "un-jammable." Radio signals operate at different frequencies along the electromagnetic spectrum. If there was some way of changing the frequency at the transmitter and receiver, the signals could pass undetected by the enemy. For it to work, the frequencies would need to change at the same time at either end—this was the tricky part. I talked about the problem with my friend George Antheil. We wanted to contribute something to the war effort and were encouraged when the government asked civilians to submit ideas to the National Inventors Council in Washington DC.

We looked at player pianos to help us with our idea. These are instruments that play themselves by "reading" cut-out dots on a piece of paper. We realized that if the transmitter and receiver both started "playing" their codes at the same time then they would work in synchronisation. We created rolls of paper with codes on them and tested them out in a special device. I called the method "frequency hopping," as it worked by letting the frequencies "hop" from one to the other. Not only did it make radio signals impossible to jam, it also meant that more devices could use the same frequencies without interfering with one another!

We took our invention to the National Inventors Council. The director was very impressed and encouraged us to develop it and prove that it could work in practice. However, the commanders of the navy couldn't be persuaded to use it.

Spying technology

• Some years later, other engineers picked up George Antheil and Hedy Lamarr's idea and developed a version that ran by electronics. This model could be made smaller and more robust, perfect for deployment. In 1962, nearly twenty years after Hedy and George developed the idea, frequency hopping was used for the first time in US defence.

• Espionage has always relied on the most up-to-date technology. Balloons, airships, high-flying jets, and orbiting satellites have been used to observe enemy activity on the ground. Telecommunications are an important military tool, but also a weak spot—tapping phone lines and cables is a central priority for espionage agencies. In modern times, the internet has helped spies gather intelligence, and computer software is used to analyze communication, find patterns, and detect individual behavior.

Mochizuki Chiyome

c. 1500s born: Japan

The best weapon a spy can have is to learn how to conceal absolutely every aspect of their actions.

I run a school for spies. The importance of concealment is one of the most crucial lessons I give. My husband, Moritoki, was a samurai lord. He was killed in battle in 1561, and I was entrusted to the care of his uncle, Takeda Shingen. Shingen was a powerful ruler with many enemies. Rival lords wanted to take over his territory, and even members of his own family tried to have him assassinated. He needed protection of the highest order. And he came to me for it.

Shingen valued the power of disguise and secrecy. Knowing his enemies would expect him to be surrounded by male warriors, he asked me to train women to protect him in secret. Free from enemy suspicion, these women would act as his hidden protection. Following Shingen's instructions, I opened a spy school in the center of Japan and recruited young women. As a cover story, I told people my school was devoted to providing religious guidance to unfortunate women. Many women had been widowed and wanted a new sense of belonging. The opportunity to seek revenge on the men who had hurt their families just made it all the sweeter for them.

中者屋

The pupils at my school were taught to be mentally strong, cunning, and resourceful. I gave lessons on how to work unseen so that they could track and follow enemies, showed them special memorization techniques so that they could recall details without writing them down, and trained them to draw out information from enemy soldiers without revealing anything. The fact that few people would suspect a young woman of being involved in espionage work made it all the easier.

My graduates were called "kunoichi" meaning "female ninja." In the decade or so that I operated my school, I built a network of around 300 kunoichi. They operated around the country, gathering intelligence, stealing secrets, and uncovering plots and military plans that would help Shingen attack his enemies. They also worked in counterintelligence, diverting enemy spies by spreading false letters and misleading rumors. They would even take part in "active measures," poisoning water supplies and carrying out assassinations.

Over time, people realized that Shingen was using female spies. However, that only added to his power. Ashamed of being continually outwitted by female spies and frightened of their effectiveness, warriors began to create myths and legends about the kunoichi. These were generally supernatural in nature. Some people believed that kunoichi could brainwash their enemies to weaken them and make them easier to defeat. I let these rumors spread. It's always helpful to make your enemies even more frightened of you than they need to be . . .

Tradecraft

•   One of the most frequently used terms by spies is "tradecraft," which refers to the skills, methods, and techniques used by people in the espionage community.

•   Examples of tradecraft include using encryption, creating a believable cover story (called a "legend" in spy circles), making dead drops, and not relying on a single source or type of intelligence.

•   As they operate with so much risk and danger, professional spies regard good tradecraft to be essential. Intelligence failures, such as the capture of a spy by the enemy or the collection of false or misleading intelligence, is often attributed to poor tradecraft.

Nathalie Sergueiew

1912–1950 born: Russia

I was born in Russia, but grew up in France. I started to work as a spy in Germany before volunteering to spy for the British. I am what they call a "double-cross" agent.

This term takes a little bit of explaining. The German intelligence service, the "Abwehr," recruit spies to work across Europe to help gather intelligence. As soon as they do so, the British make contact with the agents to insist that they work for British interests instead. The agents are warned not to tell the Germans that they have switched sides. Instead, they must keep feeding information to their handlers in Germany as if nothing has happened. That way, the British can not only prevent the German spying system from being effective, but can actually send false information to mislead and confuse the Germans. Confusing, I know. But that's the point.

It all started when I was recruited by the Abwehr. I was trained by the Abwehr officer Major Emil Kliemann, who taught me intelligence gathering and communications techniques, particularly how to use encryption to disguise my letters. My role was to travel to different parts of Europe, gather intelligence, and report my findings to him. My last mission for the Germans was in 1943, when they sent me to Spain. That was their mistake. I never truly felt loyal to the Germans, and once in Spain, I walked into a British Embassy and offered to become a spy for them.

They were wary of me at first. I was interrogated by an officer called Mary Sherer, and once they decided I was trustworthy, I was given the code name "TREASURE." Sherer became my handler. I don't like her much. Every time I see her, I think back to that first interrogation. That day she sat on the edge of a chair, arms folded and chin resting on her hands, looking at me through slightly slanted green eyes like she was examining something unpleasant. But there's no going back for me. None of them know what it's like. The danger. The paranoia. If the Germans realized that I was betraying them . . . well, it doesn't bear thinking about.

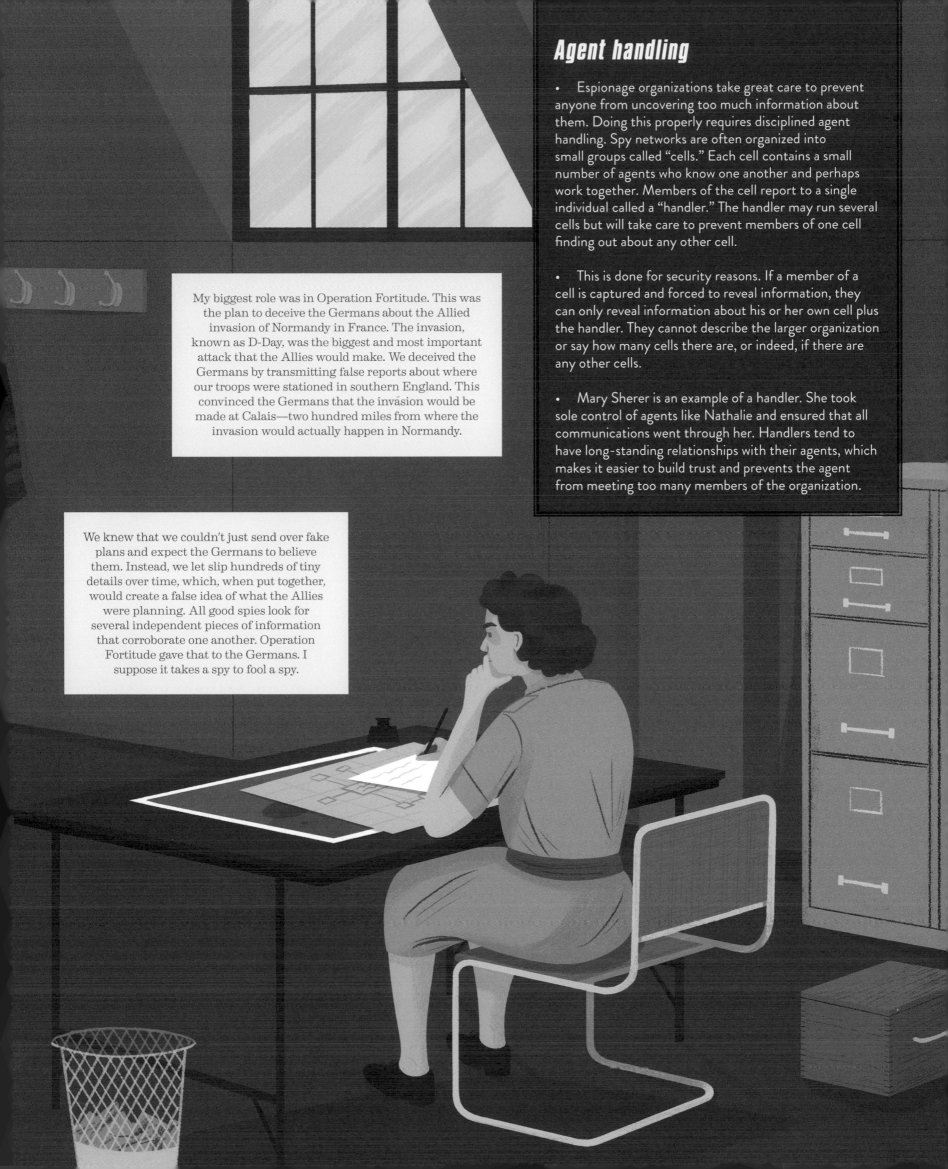

Agent handling

- Espionage organizations take great care to prevent anyone from uncovering too much information about them. Doing this properly requires disciplined agent handling. Spy networks are often organized into small groups called "cells." Each cell contains a small number of agents who know one another and perhaps work together. Members of the cell report to a single individual called a "handler." The handler may run several cells but will take care to prevent members of one cell finding out about any other cell.

- This is done for security reasons. If a member of a cell is captured and forced to reveal information, they can only reveal information about his or her own cell plus the handler. They cannot describe the larger organization or say how many cells there are, or indeed, if there are any other cells.

- Mary Sherer is an example of a handler. She took sole control of agents like Nathalie and ensured that all communications went through her. Handlers tend to have long-standing relationships with their agents, which makes it easier to build trust and prevents the agent from meeting too many members of the organization.

My biggest role was in Operation Fortitude. This was the plan to deceive the Germans about the Allied invasion of Normandy in France. The invasion, known as D-Day, was the biggest and most important attack that the Allies would make. We deceived the Germans by transmitting false reports about where our troops were stationed in southern England. This convinced the Germans that the invasion would be made at Calais—two hundred miles from where the invasion would actually happen in Normandy.

We knew that we couldn't just send over fake plans and expect the Germans to believe them. Instead, we let slip hundreds of tiny details over time, which, when put together, would create a false idea of what the Allies were planning. All good spies look for several independent pieces of information that corroborate one another. Operation Fortitude gave that to the Germans. I suppose it takes a spy to fool a spy.

Alan Turing
1912-1954 born: UK

I'd say I was a mathematician rather than call myself a spy. That's what I studied at Cambridge University. My work focuses on mathematical machines, which you might think of as early computers. It is these machines that really do the spying. However, they need highly skilled mathematicians to program them. Math is important because, at the root of it all, these things are all about solving equations and problems. My work is part of the war effort, and I work as part of a team at Bletchley Park, not far from London.

The work I do is called "cryptanalysis," which means "uncovering hidden meanings." During the Second World War, our primary goal is breaking German codes. Every bit of telecommunication is sent in code. For example, imagine the German Naval headquarters wants to send a message to one of their U-boats. They would write the message normally in "plaintext." Then they would convert it into code and transmit it to the U-boat. When the U-boat receives the message, the crew would then use their code machines to uncover the original plaintext message.

Our monitoring stations can pick up every message sent by the Germans, but we can't understand it unless we break the code. If we do this, then we could read everything that the Germans are saying to one another over the air. Attack orders, shipping movements, even full battle plans. The best part is, they wouldn't even know we're doing it!

One of my most challenging code breaking projects was the Enigma machine. This machine, used by the Germans, simply swaps each letter in a message for a different letter. Once the message is sent, a second Enigma machine can unscramble the code. The machines have three rotors, each containing letters from the entire alphabet on separate faces. The machine moves the rotors and the user can interpret the message by noting which letters are placed next to one another in the sequence. However, the machine has one small weakness. It cannot exchange one letter for another of the same type. For example, if you input the letter "E," the machine will give you a code in which any one of the other 25 letters is substituted, but not "E." It sounds insignificant, but it's actually rather important. Eliminating the unused letters is the first step to solving the entire code.

Cribs

• An important part of breaking the code comes from something called a "crib." This is a piece of confirmed plaintext that the codebreakers can use to test the accuracy of their decryptions. British intelligence officers took these from double agents, including Nathalie Sergueiew, and passed them to Turing's team. The team would compare the stolen plaintexts to their decrypted messages and check that they had made the right interpretation. The success of Bletchley Park was due to this combined intelligence effort.

We use a large machine called a "bombe" to decipher the codes. It works by imitating the process of several Enigma machines all at once. I devised a statistical method that enabled these machines to figure out which particular code an Enigma machine had made. We had to update the bombes constantly, as the Germans change their codes every two days. The work done by me and my team at Bletchley Park gave the Allies an advantage over their Axis rivals and meant that they were able to launch the invasion of Europe in 1944 and eliminate the Nazi threat. My work probably shortened the war and saved over 14 million lives. It doesn't take a genius mathematician to appreciate those numbers.

Gary Powers

1929–1977 born: USA

I'm an American pilot. I trained in the Air Force, but switched to flying for the CIA in the 1950s.

The CIA were looking for pilots to fly over the Soviet Union and take photographs of the ground. These photographs could be used by specially trained analysts to gather intelligence on military buildings and infrastructure that the Soviets were building. We weren't actually at war with the Soviets, but expected that war between our countries could break out at any time. We needed to be prepared for that. However, because we were not at war, it was especially important not to get caught. If the Soviets found out that we were spying on them, then that itself could trigger a war.

The solution to not getting caught were special planes called U-2s . These could fly very high in the sky, reaching an altitude of 69,000 feet. Getting that high takes you into the stratosphere—so high that you can see the curvature of the Earth. But needless to say, we didn't fly that high just for the incredible view. The idea was that we'd be so high up that the Soviets wouldn't be able to detect us. Even if they did, they'd be unable to attack us at that height. And if they ever claimed to have spotted one of our aircraft, our government would simply deny it or say that it was just weather-monitoring equipment.

Soon after I started work with the CIA, we learned that the Soviets had discovered that we were making these flights. However, we were convinced that they lacked the means to attack us and so we carried on. In May 1960, I flew a U-2 farther into the Soviet Union than we'd ever been before. This would prove to be a mistake. I came under attack from two enemy jets. They were unable to make a hit, but Soviet surface-to-air missiles (SAMs) fared better. One made a direct hit with my aircraft, sending my U-2 spinning at an incredible speed. The aircraft went vertical, nose-up, and I struggled to operate the ejection procedure. I had instructions to activate a self-destruct device on the plane if this ever happened so that the Soviets wouldn't be able to examine it. However, I couldn't do this in time, and separately, the U-2 and I plummeted all the way to Earth.

Fortunately, I survived the descent by parachute. Unfortunately, most of my plane survived the fall too. I was taken to prison for interrogation. The Soviets had been able to recover the camera equipment from the U-2, and it was obvious what I had been doing. I was made to publicly admit to being involved in espionage and apologize for this crime. This was a deliberate move. It made the Americans look bad to the Soviet people. We were presented as devious criminals who wanted to ignore the fact that our countries were officially at peace with one another. It was also a show of strength, as the Soviets were now able to say, "We have the technology to shoot down even your highest aircraft. You can't get away with these flights."

Disavowal

• When an agency sends a spy into hostile territory, it often tells them that, should they be caught, it will deny all knowledge of them. Even if the spy admits to being a paid agent, the agency will claim never to have heard of the spy before and to be unaware of their actions. This is called disavowal, and it is done so that the country does not have to admit that it has been spying on its rival. However, in cases such as that of Gary Powers, there is other evidence that the mission was official espionage.

I was found guilty and sentenced to ten years in a prison near Moscow. Meanwhile, the political fall-out rumbled on. The incident made relations difficult between our US president, Dwight D. Eisenhower, and his Soviet counterpart. For a while, people even worried that it might lead to outright war. However, the US government were able to resolve the situation. The FBI had captured a Soviet agent, Rudolf Abel, who had been spying in the United States. It was clear that our countries were as guilty as each other. Following some careful negotiations, an agreement to "swap" prisoners was made. Abel would be returned to the Soviet Union, and I would go back to the USA. Just under two years after crashing, I made it home.

Policarpa Salavarrieta

1795–1817 born: Colombia

Names are not important. I have gone by many. The Spanish Royalists call me their enemy. I call myself a revolutionary.

I was born to a large family in New Grenada, which would later be called Colombia. My early childhood was happy, and I was close to my brothers and sisters, especially my little brother Bibiano. But that all changed in 1802 when a smallpox epidemic killed both my parents, along with two of my siblings. The tragedy split my family apart. Many of my siblings moved away, while Bibiano and I, along with our eldest sister, went to live with our godmother. I wish it had never happened, but it taught me at a young age not to take security for granted and how to remain strong even when you are afraid. Lessons I would not forget.

Although in South America, my country had been ruled by Spain for many years. People wanted freedom from Spain, and in 1810, we proudly declared independence. However, five years later, Spain sought to recapture our country and a terrible war broke out. I knew then that I must join the revolutionary movement and defeat the Spanish. I was only around 19 or 20 years old at the time, which gave me certain advantages. The revolutionaries were mostly young men who were unable to carry out their missions in the open. However, as a young woman, I could move around the city, gathering intelligence free of suspicion.

I offered my skills as a seamstress to rich people who were supporters of the Spanish king. I saw them as traitors, but I pretended to be nice to them as I set about repairing their clothes. They thought very little of me and probably didn't think I was intelligent enough to understand their conversations. But I kept my eyes and ears open all the time. Working undetected, I gathered all kinds of intelligence. I memorized overheard details, learning about plans that the Royal Army was making. I was even able to find out what they knew about the revolutionaries. It was an incomplete picture, but every item of information helped us.

Despite our care, the reality was that we were all living in danger. We couldn't evade capture forever and soon, the arrests began. Among the first to be caught was Ambrosio Almeyda—a revolutionary leader. He knew an incredible amount about our work, which put us all in danger. If he gave in to their interrogations, then we would all be captured. Then my fellow revolutionary Alejo Sabaraín was arrested. He had a list of revolutionary patriots with him at the time of his arrest and my name was on it. There would be no escape for me.

Sergeant Iglesias, a Spanish officer, was sent to arrest me. Seeing the soldiers arrive, I immediately gathered all papers relating to our organization and threw them in the kitchen fire. Iglesias suspected nothing, and I had prevented further leaks of information. Bibiano and I were then taken to a prison for questioning. I told them nothing about my work for the revolution, but nonetheless we were sentenced to death for treason. But I don't call it treason, I call it patriotism. Names might not be important, but beliefs are, and I am proud to die as a patriot.

Revolutionary spies

• A revolution is an event in which a group of organized people overthrow a government and start controlling the country for themselves. There have been many revolutions in history and they are often times of intrigue and violence. Revolutionary spies have roles that include gathering intelligence on the government's strengths and weaknesses, recruiting new members to the revolutionary group, and working with foreign powers that would also like to see the government toppled. Revolutionary groups are also major targets for government spies. In some cases, soldiers or police officers are sent to pose as revolutionaries to gather intelligence and disrupt the group. Certain agents have a special mission of persuading the group to commit crimes so that they can be arrested and their activities halted. These people are known as agents provocateurs.

Nancy Wake
1912–2011 born: New Zealand

I was born in New Zealand but grew up in Australia. Life was pretty quiet and I always hungered for adventure.

At 16, I ran away from home to London, where I became a journalist. From there I toured Europe, reporting on everything I could see. At the time Europe was in political turmoil. The Nazis had come to power and so I reported on their activities. I wanted to show the world how terrible they were. Doing so also gave me useful experience in gathering and analyzing information. It was while living in Europe that I met a wealthy businessman named Henri Fiocca. We fell in love and started our married life in the French city of Marseille. Our future looked assured with so much to look forward to. But then the Nazis got in the way again.

The Nazis invaded France in 1940. Some of us, Henri and I included, formed a resistance, determined to clear them out of France. In those early days, one of our most important tasks was getting British soldiers out of France. Some of them had become trapped there, and the Nazis were trying to capture them. My role was to help them escape and get back to Britain, where they could help to start a major attack on the Nazis. I worked as a courier, supporting the secret network that helped the soldiers. I was so good at this that the Gestapo (the Nazi secret police), started calling me the "White Mouse." They announced that anyone who captured me would get five million francs as a reward.

The Gestapo did everything they could to catch me, but I outwitted them at every turn. However, eventually the danger became too great, and I was forced to escape to Britain, where I joined the Special Operations Executive (SOE). This was a new organization set up by the British to operate in secret throughout occupied Europe. SOE agents were highly trained in techniques of espionage, combat, and surveillance. I was trained in the SOE's techniques, excelling in them all and impressing my instructors. It did not take long for me to be assigned to a mission. One that would take me back to France.

I arrived in France via parachute, descending into the Forest of Troncais. I landed in a tree, but thankfully was cut down by the local resistance units who had been sent to meet me. Working in enemy-held territory is a constant struggle. It was exhausting, intense, and—needless to say—deadly. My goal was to make it more dangerous for the Nazis than it was for us. To that end, I led raids on enemy targets, demolished bridges to make it difficult for them to get around the country, and even attacked them outright. The main Allied force was not scheduled to attack for several months, but I had no intention of wasting time.

Of course, the most important part of my role was espionage. This meant maintaining the flow of intelligence from France to Allied headquarters in southern England. The intelligence was transmitted by radio, using secret codes. On one occasion, the codes got lost in a raid. I couldn't just stand idly by, so I rode almost 200 miles on a bicycle to reach another radio operator and contact headquarters. For me, every victory, no matter how small, or how hard-won, mattered. I was just pleased that I was able to do so much for the war effort. We won, of course.

The Second World War

• Almost every country was involved in some way in the Second World War. The Allies comprised the UK (and its empire), the United States, Canada, Australia, and France. The Axis powers were Germany, Italy, and Japan, along with their supporters. It is estimated that almost 60 million people were killed. Like the First World War, each side tried to gain a decisive advantage by developing more powerful weapons. In 1945, the United States successfully developed a powerful new type of bomb, called an atomic bomb. Although it was created with a high degree of secrecy, spies managed to discover the development of it. This led to a strange situation in which the US vice president didn't know about the bomb, but the leader of the Soviet Union did.

John Edgar Hoover

1895–1972 born: USA

I am the most powerful man in America. Bold claim? Perhaps. But I have always known that knowledge is power, and no one—not even the president— knows as much as me. I am the director of the Federal Bureau of Intelligence (FBI). My organization is mainly focused on law enforcement, but we also have responsibility for counterespionage. As far as I'm concerned, it's all crime. It doesn't matter to me whether you're a spy or a regular lawbreaker; I have you in my sights.

I have devoted my career to the destruction of communism. The challenging thing about communism is that it is a belief. Anyone can become a communist, which means anyone can become my enemy—even my fellow Americans. Our main target is groups. A single communist is a nuisance, but groups are a threat. My agents spy on groups like the Communist Party USA and look for weak members whom we can convince to give us information. Some of my agents even join organizations to obtain intelligence on them. Our first goal is to create division in the organization itself, sowing doubt and causing arguments. A divided organization is a weak organization, and that's just how I like it.

After the Second World War, I led an FBI scheme called COINTELPRO (Counter Intelligence Program). It expanded our anti-communist work so that we could target more groups. We went after "obvious" targets such as the Communist Party, but also after civil-rights groups, anti-war organizations, and the American Indian Movement. Once I set a target, my men would disrupt and harass the group. They broke into headquarters and homes, looking for incriminating items such as weapons and documents. If they found anything, they'd use it as an excuse to make an arrest. If they found nothing, they would plant something and come back and make an arrest.

Red scares

- For most of the 20th century, the world's most powerful countries were divided by ideology. In the United States, capitalism was seen as the best way to run things, while in the Soviet Union, communism was the preferred system. Officials in the USA were concerned that Americans might, with the aid of Soviet spies, turn to communism. At two critical moments, just after the First and Second World Wars, fears of communism ran particularly high. As the color red is associated with communism, these periods became know as "red scares." American intelligence agencies were concerned with the activities of American sympathizers to communism and secret agents from communist countries. They called these people "subversives" and went to great lengths to control them. It was difficult to tell who was a real subversive, and many innocent people got caught up in the red scare, losing their jobs, their security, and, in some cases, enduring imprisonment.

This constant pursuit of targets drew in a lot of useful intelligence. I gathered files on thousands of Americans, even famous ones, from celebrities to presidents. Among the most valuable items of intelligence is anything that might embarrass the target. Let's say they have a dark secret, perhaps they are a cheat or have committed a crime. I gather proof of it and let them know that I have it. They know that if they cross me, I will tell everyone about their little secret. You can only imagine how scared this makes people. I will use anything to achieve my goals.

J. EDGAR HOOVER

Is this what spying is meant to be about? Most people would say no. My actions are not about keeping America safe, or fighting crime or winning wars. For me, running an espionage agency is about power and control.

Harold "Kim" Philby

1912–1988 born: India

My name is Harold Philby, but everybody calls me "Kim." Except for the Soviets. They call me by the code names "Sonny" or "Stanley." I have code names because I am a spy. I was born in India, when it was part of the British Empire. Later, I attended Trinity College, Cambridge, and it was there that I made a group of friends who would change my life forever. I won't tell you everything about our group—I am a spy after all! But I'll admit that there were four of us: Guy Burgess, Anthony Blunt, Donald MacLean, and me. We were all on course to have successful lives, but the political system in our country seemed cold and cruel to us. In college, we came to admire the Soviet system. Their ideology, called Marxism, seemed fairer and we believed it would be better if the Soviet system spread to the rest of the world. When we were asked, in total secrecy, if we would help push the Soviet system, we all agreed. Even though it meant betraying Britain.

Our mission was to pretend to be loyal to the British government while secretly passing intelligence to the Soviet Union. We took jobs in the diplomatic service, the foreign office, and, in my case, the Secret Service. These roles gave us access to lots of official secrets, including military plans and information about the government. We took pictures of documents using a special camera called a Minox, and thousands of notes, contracts, plans, and maps made their way into Soviet hands because of us. On a few occasions, we were told to slow things down. We provided so much high-quality intelligence that the Soviet leaders started to think that it must have been fake. They thought we might even have been triple agents, only pretending to be disloyal to Britain to fool the Soviets!

Of course, we couldn't remain hidden forever. In 1951, I heard through my secret spy channels that MacLean was under suspicion. I couldn't protect him, but I could warn him. He and Burgess decided to flee to Moscow, where they would be welcomed as heroes. As far as the British were concerned, they had simply disappeared. This was hugely embarrassing for the British government. It was obvious that allowing spies to get so close to the heart of power was a colossal failure of intelligence. Even our allies no longer trusted us. As a longtime friend of Burgess, I fell under suspicion, but no action was taken. I was, however, made to resign as a British spy.

I found work as a journalist, but I never really left the world of espionage. I continued to gather intelligence and pass it to MI6. It was while doing this that I heard once again that I was under suspicion. I was in Beirut in Lebanon when I got a tip that MI6 suspected me of working for the Soviets and that they were sending someone to check on me. I had no time to lose. There was a ship leaving Beirut for the Soviet Union that morning. With help from my Soviet handlers, I boarded the ship and we forced it to leave early before any British agents could identify me. In Britain, I was condemned a traitor and could never return. I would live for the rest of my life in Moscow, a lonely former spy.

The Cold War

• The Cold War is the name given to a pattern of global tensions that existed from just after the end of the Second World War in 1945, until the collapse of the Soviet Union in 1991. The world's most powerful countries formed large "blocs," with capitalist countries, led by the United States on one side, and communist countries, led by the Soviet Union, on the other.

• Both sides had access to nuclear weapons and were reluctant to go to war against each other directly. As a result, the "war" became more about uncovering the other side's secrets and seeking to undermine the enemy from the inside. Spies became especially important in this era.

• The pressures of the Cold War prompted both sides to develop ever more sophisticated spying techniques. Some of this was highly technological and involved innovations such as the U-2 spy plane and, later on, spy satellites in orbit around the Earth. However, most Cold War espionage was performed by people on the ground. Both sides feared that their own people would betray them and work for the other side. This happened many times, and some of the most famous incidents of the Cold War involved betrayal.

Mata Hari

1876–1917 born: Netherlands

I'm remembered both as a spy and as a dancer. I was a good dancer, one of the most famous in the world.

But I wasn't an amazing spy and funnily enough it is as a spy that I'm best remembered. When I was young my family were quite wealthy, but that all changed in my teenage years when my father went bankrupt and my mother died. My family fell apart and I began to drift through life. I felt most at home in wealthy circles and married a man with a lot of money. We moved to the Dutch East Indies (Indonesia) and lived a life that was luxurious but unhappy.

After my marriage ended, I moved back to Europe and started my career as a dancer. I took the name "Mata Hari," which is a Malay term that means "Eye of the Day." It made me sound more exotic than my real name, Margaretha. With my exotic style and dancing talents, I became famous. Life was good once more—even more so when I met the love of my life, Captain Vadim Maslov, a dashing Russian pilot.

When the First World War broke out in 1914, Vadim went to France to fight against the Germans. He was seriously injured in aerial combat and I wanted desperately to be by his side. However, the French authorities would not let me see him unless I agreed to spy for them. As a Dutch national, I was from a neutral country and could travel more easily between France and Germany. The French also knew that I had contacts in German high society and asked me to use these to gather intelligence for them. I wanted to see Vadim, so what choice did I have? My handler in French intelligence was Captain Georges Ladoux. I had to work closely with him, though I don't think he ever liked me much. He told me that my target was the German crown prince Wilhelm, whom I had known before the war. He was now acting as a general in the German Army. My job was to rekindle our friendship and steal secrets from him.

The First World War

• The First World War was a global conflict that lasted from 1914 to 1918. Groups of countries formed alliances to fight one another. One side were the Central Powers, comprising Germany, Austria-Hungary, the Ottoman Empire, and Bulgaria. On the other side were France, the United Kingdom (plus their empires, including Canada, Australia, India, New Zealand, Algeria, and Senegal), Russia (until 1917), and the United States (from 1917). For most of the war, the powers were evenly matched and sought every possible advantage. Spying was an essential part of the plans on both sides. Agents were deployed in enemy territory to gather intelligence, telecommunications were intercepted, and both sides tried to create political trouble in the homelands of the enemy in an effort to weaken their fighting strength.

My first step in getting to the crown prince was to make contact with a German officer named Major Kalle. He recognized my value as a spy for Germany and offered me money to share secrets of the French plans. I agreed and told him that I'd give him all the information I could. Privately, I knew that this wouldn't be of much use. All I knew was gossip, but I felt trapped between two great powers. If I'm honest, I was a little out of my depth. I never planned to become a spy—it was a role I was forced into.

The Germans weren't impressed with the intelligence I gave them. They discussed my espionage work over their radio communications, even though they knew the French were listening in. They made it obvious that they were talking about me and used the code name H-21, which made it look like I was a full German spy! They let the French arrest me and I was put on trial. The French announced to everyone that I was a spy— it covered up some of the mistakes that they had made, and as I was not French myself, it meant that French people could be cleared of blame. I'm no spy, not a real one anyway, but I am, sadly, a scapegoat. The sentence of the court was death.

Noor Inayat Khan

1914–1944 born: Russia

I'm a wireless operator in one of the most treacherous and deadly environments in the history of warfare.

I never expected to end up like this. I was born in Moscow to an Indian father and an American mother. We moved to France and although my father died when I was only 13, my childhood was a happy one. I was especially close to my younger brother, Vilayat. He and I saw the world in the same way, believing that killing was wrong, even if it meant putting yourself in danger to avoid having to do it. When the Second World War broke out in 1939, this belief remained very strongly in my mind.

When Germany invaded France, my family fled to England, where I was determined to join the war effort and stop the Nazi advance. So, I trained as a wireless operator (WO). The wireless systems had to go where the action was, which meant that some WOs had to travel into enemy territory. I volunteered to go. This meant receiving additional training on how to cope in the deadly environment, including the use of secret codes and concealment. The worst part was the interrogation training. I would be at risk of capture, and—as a WO—would have firsthand knowledge of our missions. The instructors subjected me to realistic interrogation, using techniques to frighten and disorient me. I almost couldn't stand it, but I had made a commitment and I intended to keep it.

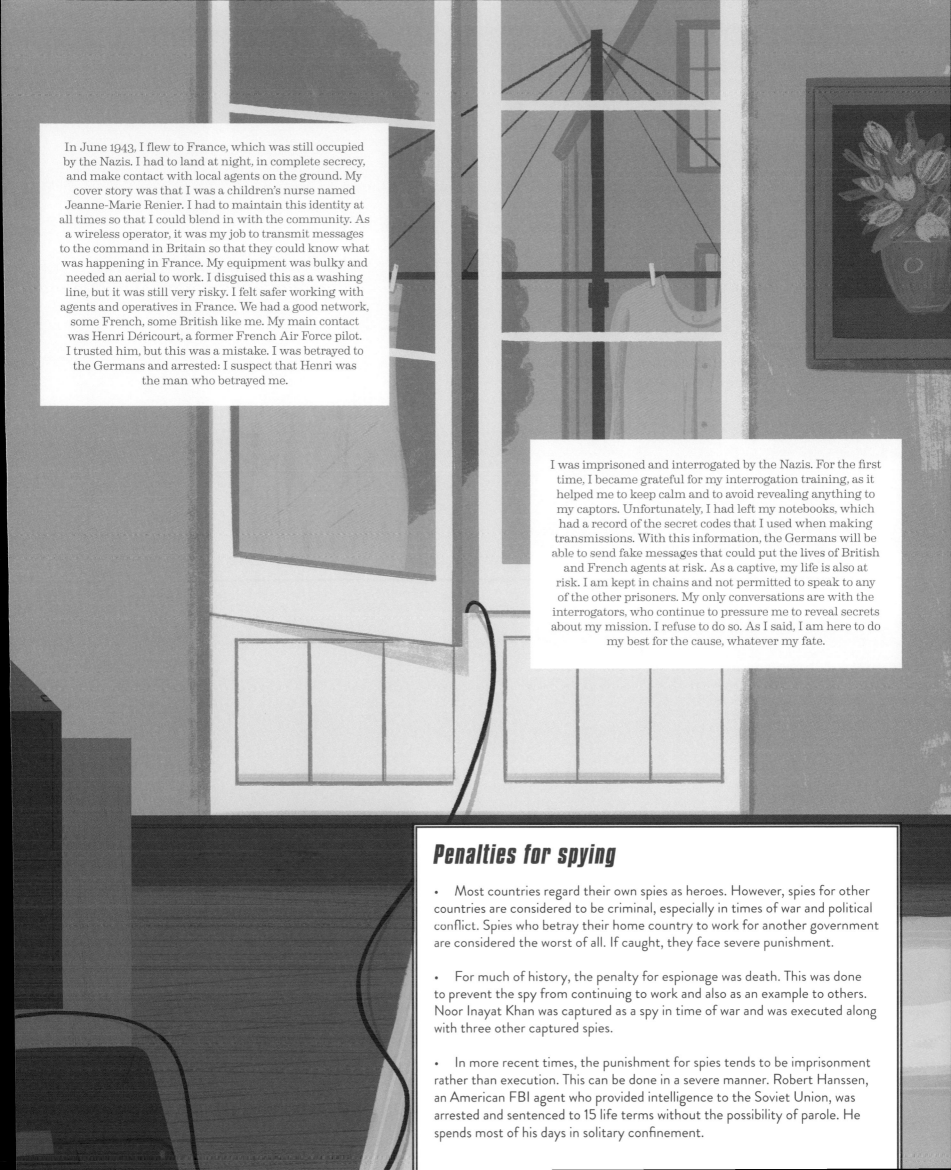

In June 1943, I flew to France, which was still occupied by the Nazis. I had to land at night, in complete secrecy, and make contact with local agents on the ground. My cover story was that I was a children's nurse named Jeanne-Marie Renier. I had to maintain this identity at all times so that I could blend in with the community. As a wireless operator, it was my job to transmit messages to the command in Britain so that they could know what was happening in France. My equipment was bulky and needed an aerial to work. I disguised this as a washing line, but it was still very risky. I felt safer working with agents and operatives in France. We had a good network, some French, some British like me. My main contact was Henri Déricourt, a former French Air Force pilot. I trusted him, but this was a mistake. I was betrayed to the Germans and arrested: I suspect that Henri was the man who betrayed me.

I was imprisoned and interrogated by the Nazis. For the first time, I became grateful for my interrogation training, as it helped me to keep calm and to avoid revealing anything to my captors. Unfortunately, I had left my notebooks, which had a record of the secret codes that I used when making transmissions. With this information, the Germans will be able to send fake messages that could put the lives of British and French agents at risk. As a captive, my life is also at risk. I am kept in chains and not permitted to speak to any of the other prisoners. My only conversations are with the interrogators, who continue to pressure me to reveal secrets about my mission. I refuse to do so. As I said, I am here to do my best for the cause, whatever my fate.

Penalties for spying

• Most countries regard their own spies as heroes. However, spies for other countries are considered to be criminal, especially in times of war and political conflict. Spies who betray their home country to work for another government are considered the worst of all. If caught, they face severe punishment.

• For much of history, the penalty for espionage was death. This was done to prevent the spy from continuing to work and also as an example to others. Noor Inayat Khan was captured as a spy in time of war and was executed along with three other captured spies.

• In more recent times, the punishment for spies tends to be imprisonment rather than execution. This can be done in a severe manner. Robert Hanssen, an American FBI agent who provided intelligence to the Soviet Union, was arrested and sentenced to 15 life terms without the possibility of parole. He spends most of his days in solitary confinement.

Oleg Gordievsky
1938- born: Russia

I was born in the Soviet Union but it collapsed in the early 1990s, bringing an end to the Cold War, which had dominated so much of my life.

Still, I have chosen to remain in Britain, the country for which I have worked for a long time. I'm Oleg Gordievsky, and I was a Cold War spy. Back in my youth, I was an enthusiastic Soviet. I joined the Committee for State Security in 1963. This organization was better known by its Russian initials, KGB. It was one of the most professional and feared espionage organizations in history. The training was tough, the discipline hard, and officers like me had to show absolute loyalty to the organization and the Soviet state. It was a large and powerful organization. The KGB was in charge of all espionage and intelligence security for the entire Soviet Union. In short, we spied on foreigners and our own citizens alike. This gave us enormous power.

KGB officers worked in Soviet embassies around the world. Officially, we were there as honest diplomats, but our real mission was to gather intelligence. Our embassy offices were known as rezidentura or "residencies." We used them as hubs for gathering and analyzing intelligence. I worked hard at the rezidentura, but I soon grew suspicious of the Soviet regime. I disliked the way the regime leaders sought to oppress and control people, including those of other countries that bordered the Union. I no longer wanted to work for the Soviet Union. In fact, I wanted to bring it down. That's how I came to work for the British government. I met with the British Secret Intelligence Service (MI6) and agreed to continue working for the KGB. But I was just pretending to be loyal. In reality, I would use my KGB position to gather intelligence that I could secretly pass to the British. I was to become a double agent. Unaware of my real loyalties, my KGB bosses promoted me to the rezidentura in London. My role was to gather intelligence on the British and pass it to the Soviets. As somebody secretly loyal to Britain, I was able to provide the Soviets only with information that the British deemed harmless.

Fictional spies

- The intrigue, danger, and adventurousness of a spy's life has made it an attractive topic for writers of fiction. Spies appear in ancient legends and are often featured in Hollywood movies and in computer games.

- To make these stories exciting, the lives of fictional spies are often more thrilling than those of their real-life counterparts. Spies such as James Bond are presented as multi-skilled, tough, and charismatic, and their work takes them all over the world, often to the planet's most exotic locations.

- Some writers have tried to portray espionage as rather less exciting. George Smiley, the lead character in a series of novels by the British writer (and ex-spy!) John le Carré, is described as an older figure, short, somewhat overweight, and ordinary looking. In Smiley's world, spies are often unhappy and troubled because of the lies they are required to tell and the effect that their work has on their personal lives.

It's lonely work, being a double agent. I could never rest easy and suspected that I was being watched at all times by the KGB. And I was right to be suspicious. In 1985, I was summoned very suddenly back to Moscow. On arrival, I was arrested and subjected to questioning. Although it could not be proven that I had betrayed my country, it was made clear that the KGB no longer trusted me. I was released but forbidden from leaving the Soviet Union. The KGB continued to watch me wherever I went in Moscow. I was desperate to leave. But how?

Fortunately, I had agreed an escape plan with MI6. I was to wait on a specific street corner at 7:00 p.m., carrying a bag from the British supermarket Safeway. If I saw a man also carrying a bag from a British shop, then the signal would be complete. I was so nervous, but at 7:00 p.m. I saw a man with a bag from Harrods in London. We made no hint of recognition other than eye contact, but the signal had been set. A few days later, I went out for a run and as usual was followed by KGB men. However, I knew their tricks and was able to escape. I got onto a train and headed for the border where I was met by MI6 officers. I had made my escape. Since then, I have remained in the UK.

Sidney Reilly
c. 1873–1925 born: Russia

I am probably the world's greatest liar.
I move easily between names, identities, and nationalities, adopting whichever is most useful to me at any given time. I was born in the Russian Empire, but I have spent most of my life traveling. Some people call me the "Ace of Spies." I have worked for several different espionage organizations in many countries, but I feel no particular loyalty to any of them. My main motivation is adventure. It has been a very interesting life, whether or not you believe my tales.

Adventure is wonderful, but it's no good without money. Luckily, I've been able to combine the two. Britain's Special Branch police paid me in return for secret information on my fellow Russians. Later, the Japanese did the same. Russia and Japan went to war with each other in 1905, and the Japanese intelligence service was desperate for details of Russian planning and capabilities. Loving money more than Russia, I happily provided them with it. Did it bother me that I was betraying my homeland to two different powers? Not in the least.

The First World War broke out in 1914, which presented a lot of opportunities for a man like me. I spent much of the war in New York, running a business that made weapons. The best part was, as America was neutral, I was able to sell weapons to both sides. At least for a while. In 1917, America declared war on Germany, which meant that I was unable to sell weapons to them. Later that year, Russia had a revolution and left the war. I was left without customers, but there were still bigger opportunities to come.

The Russian Revolution

• Russia had been ruled for centuries by powerful emperors known as tsars. Although they had a lot of control over the country, many people were poor and were opposed to their rule. In 1917, Nicholas II, the last tsar, was removed from power in a revolution. This led to a major crisis, and ultimately, a new type of government took over. This government, led by a group called the Bolsheviks, was opposed to the First World War and took Russia out of it. The Allied forces, led by France, Britain, and the United States, lost a war ally and were opposed to the Bolsheviks. They sent soldiers and ships to try to prevent the Bolsheviks from taking over, and used men like Sidney Reilly to stir up trouble. These efforts failed and Bolshevik Russia took over several neighboring countries and set up a new power called the Soviet Union. The Soviet Union was treated with suspicion by Western countries, and although they became allies in the Second World War, this suspicion would remain until the Soviet Union fell apart in 1991.

I adopted yet another identity and got a job with the Bolshevik secret police, the Cheka. This gave me access to people I hoped to persuade to attack the leadership. One such man was Eduard Berzin. I tried to convince him to switch sides, but he was a loyal Bolshevik. Pretending to go along with my schemes, he reported me to the authorities. Unaware of this, I continued with a secret plot to assassinate the Bolshevik leader, Vladimir Lenin. The plot was in place when I found out that somebody else had shot Lenin, who was injured but alive. Thanks to Berzin, suspicion fell on me, but I used my secret identity to slip through police checks and escape to London. By then, I was famous as the man who tried to overthrow the Russian government.

Russia was in the middle of a civil war at this time. Two groups, the Whites and the Reds, fought one another to take over the country. The Allied powers, which included Britain and America, supported the Whites and sent troops to help them in their efforts. With my Russian background, I was ideally suited to help in this mission. I traveled to Russia to meet with White leaders and give them support. With my trademark deviousness, I also met with soldiers from the Red side and offered them money to switch loyalties. I grew confident in my skills as an agitator and prepared a scheme to capture the Bolshevik leaders and overthrow the government.

Zheng Pingru

1918–1940   born: China

I am proud to call myself Chinese. Although I'm half Japanese — my mother was born there and taught me to speak the language fluently — my heart is in China.

A lot of these feelings come from my dad. He's just as proudly Chinese too and we all want to see China become strong again. Because of this, I have spent most of my life worrying about Japan. My dad had long feared that they wanted to take over China and rule it for their own purposes. When I was only 13, his worries proved true and Japanese soldiers invaded a northern part of the country called Manchuria, treating the citizens appallingly and bringing violence and terror to the streets.

The fighting continued for many years, and I spent a lot of time taking part in protests against the Japanese. We knew that they would not stop until they had taken over the whole country. I felt that it was my duty to stand up to this. But at the same time, I knew I must lead my own life. I enrolled in college and performed in drama in my spare time. However, this all came to an end when the Japanese attacked my part of China in 1937. My life as a carefree student ended and my career as a spy began. But I had a major advantage in my new role — I could speak the language of the invaders and knew a lot about their culture. Working for the Kuomintang (the Chinese nationalist movement), I traveled through the streets of Shanghai, listening in and observing the activities of the Japanese soldiers. They talked freely in Japanese, never considering that I could understand their every word.

Any Chinese person who collaborated with the Japanese was a traitor in my eyes. The worst one was Ding Mocun, who acted as the security chief for the collaborating Chinese. We called him the Butcher because of the way he treated the brave fighters of the resistance. The Kuomintang wanted him gone and gave me the job of setting a trap for him. I had actually known him before the war began — he had been my headmaster in school — and I was instructed to exploit this connection. So, very carefully, I arranged to "accidentally" bump into him. I used intelligence from my fellow spies to find out where he would be and made up a reason to be there myself. Over time, I gained his trust and eventually I became his girlfriend.

Spending time with Ding gave me more opportunities to gather intelligence. I continued, at great personal risk, to communicate with Kuomintang agents and keep them informed. We formed a plan to stop his activities once and for all. One evening, Ding and I were visiting his friend's house for dinner and we would come home along Nanjing Road, a busy shopping street. It was perfect for our plans. I asked Ding to help me choose a new coat. We got out at the pre-arranged spot, and I pretended to look at coats while keeping an eye out for the Kuomintang assassins. I spotted them, but unfortunately so did Ding. He realized what was going on and ran back to the car. His driver jumped on the pedals, and the car disappeared into the night.

A question of loyalty

• Many spies are recruited forcefully and are made to hand over intelligence out of fear of violence or blackmail. Others seek financial reward and effectively "sell" secrets to anyone who is able to pay for them. In modern times, people seek out careers in intelligence services as they might in any other profession. However, some of the most effective spies in history have acted out of commitment or loyalty to a cause. They put themselves in danger because they believe in the mission. Such spies are successful because they have a loyalty to their own side that means they cannot be bought off or persuaded to switch sides. Zheng is an example of such a spy. She had a belief in the Chinese cause that meant she was prepared to risk her life to further its aims.

The plan had failed entirely. With a lengthy operation like this, you only get one chance at success, and with just one mistake, the work of several months can disappear in an instant. I had done my part well, earning Ding's trust and delivering him to the agreed location, but I was to be punished for the failure of my fellow agents. Ding knew I was in on the plot and had me arrested for espionage. My sentence? Well, there's only one outcome for a spy caught like me. At least I can die knowing that I did my best for China.

GLOSSARY

Agency
An organization.

Agent
A spy.

Agent provocateur
Someone who persuades a person or group to commit a crime so they can be arrested and their activities stopped.

Agitator
Someone who stirs up others to further a cause.

Allied Forces (World War II)
The nations that formally united to fight against the Axis in World War II, including the UK, France, the Soviet Union, and the USA.

Allied Powers (World War I)
The nations that fought against the Central Powers during World War I, including France, the UK, Russia (until 1917), and the USA (from 1917).

Atomic bomb
A weapon with violent explosive power, which comes from the sudden release of energy resulting from the splitting of nuclei of a heavy chemical element (such as plutonium or uranium).

Axis Powers (World War II)
The countries aligned against the Allied Forces in World War II, including Germany, Italy, and Japan.

Capitalism
A system where a country's trade and industry are controlled by private owners for profit and not by the country's government.

Central Powers (World War I)
The countries aligned against the Allied Powers in World War I, comprising Germany, Austria-Hungary, the Ottoman Empire, and Bulgaria.

CIA
The Central Intelligence Agency, the USA's foreign intelligence gathering service.

Cipher
A code that substitutes one letter for another.

Civilian
Someone who is not in the armed services or the police force.

Code
A way of disguising a message by replacing words with other letters and/or numbers.

Codebreaker
Someone who solves codes.

Cold War
A time of tension between the Soviet Union and its allies and the USA and its allies. The Cold War lasted from after the Second World War until the collapse of the Soviet Union in 1991 and was called "cold" because there was no direct fighting between the two sides.

Communism
A system where property and goods are shared and the government controls production.

Confederacy
During the American Civil War (1861–65), a group of southern slave-holding states who rebelled and left the rest of the United States.

Conflict
A serious disagreement or argument.

Conspirator
Someone who takes part in a secret plan or plot.

Counterintelligence
Action taken by spies to work against a danger or threat from enemy spies and prevent them from finding out their secrets.

Crib
A section of an encoded message that can easily be turned into plaintext and so understood. This can then help a cryptographer crack the entire code.

Cryptographer
Someone who studies or uses secret writing systems such as codes and ciphers.

Double agent
A spy who pretends to work for someone while really working for their enemy.

Drop
The way two spies pass items or information. A dead drop is when two spies do not meet directly, but leave information in a secret location.

Empire
A group of countries ruled over by one country.

Encryption
The process of turning information into a secret code so that only authorized people can read it.

Engineer
Someone whose job it is to design, build, or maintain engines, machines, or structures.

Espionage
Spying.

Handler
Someone whose job it is to manage spies.

Headquarters
Somewhere occupied by a military commander and their staff.

Infrastructure
The basic services a country needs, such as roads, transportation, and power supplies.

Inscrutable
Difficult to investigate or understand.

Intelligence
Knowledge or information about a situation, particularly about an enemy or possible enemy.

Invasion
The act of invading a country or region with armed forces.

Legend
A spy's made-up background or cover story, usually supported by fake documents.

Marxism
The communist ideas of the German writer Karl Marx (1818–83).

Patriotism
Love for your country.

Plaintext
A message in its original form before it has been encrypted.

Revolution
When a large group of people in a country rise up to overthrow the government and demand change.

Royal pardon
An official order by a king or queen to stop the punishment of a person accused of a crime or offence.

Satellite
Something that is placed in orbit around the Earth or another planet to collect information or for communication.

Soviet Union
A country that existed between 1922 and 1991 and was made up of 15 states.

Spy
Someone employed by a government or other organization to secretly get information on an enemy or competitor.

Spymaster
Someone who leads espionage activities.

Spy ring
A group of spies working together.

Target
The person, object, or place selected for investigation or attack.

Territory
An area of land that belongs to a ruler or state.

Terrorism
The use of violence and fear for political or religious reasons.

Tradecraft
The skills, methods, and techniques used by spies.

Treacherous
Something that is dangerously unstable and unpredictable.

U-boat
A military submarine used by Germany in the two world wars.

Union
During the American Civil War (1861–65), the northern states who stayed loyal to the United States.

Warfare
Conflict between opposing sides.

Inspiring | Educating | Creating | Entertaining

Brimming with creative inspiration, how-to projects, and useful information to enrich your everyday life, Quarto Knows is a favorite destination for those pursuing their interests and passions. Visit our site and dig deeper with our books into your area of interest: Quarto Creates, Quarto Cooks, Quarto Homes, Quarto Lives, Quarto Drives, Quarto Explores, Quarto Gifts, or Quarto Kids.

First Published in 2020 by Wide Eyed Editions,
an imprint of The Quarto Group.
100 Cummings Center, Suite 265D, Beverly, MA 01915, USA.
T +1 978-282-9590 F +1 978-283-2742 **www.QuartoKnows.com**

ISBN 978-0-7112-4756-7
eISBN 978-0-7112-5814-3

The illustrations were created digitally
Set in Brandon Grotesque, Centennial, Compacta, Eames Century Modern

Published by Georgia Amson-Bradshaw
Designed by Sasha Moxon
Edited by Claire Grace
Production by Dawn Cameron

Manufactured in Maribor, Slovenia DZ052020

9 8 7 6 5 4 3 2